THE CHANGING YEARS
MY CHOICES AND DECISIONS

by
Corinne Sanders, O.P., M.S.
Judy Bisignano, O.P., Ed.D.

illustrated by Kay Mirocha

Cover by Kathryn Hyndman

Copyright © Good Apple, Inc., 1987

ISBN No. 0-86653-421-0

Printing No. 987654321

GOOD APPLE, INC.
BOX 299
CARTHAGE, IL 62321-0299

The purchase of this book entitles the buyer to duplicate the student activity pages for classroom use only. Any other use requires written permission from Good Apple, Inc.

All rights reserved. Printed in the United States of America.

DESCRIPTION OF KINO LEARNING CENTER

Kino Learning Center is a private, nonprofit elementary and secondary school founded in Tucson, Arizona, in 1975 by parents seeking an alternative learning environment for children. The school is staffed by 20 teachers and has an enrollment of 160 students between the ages of 3 and 18.

Within the prepared learning environment of the school, each child is free to choose from worthwhile options, a sequence of activities unique to his/her needs and experiences, and in which he/she finds success, interest and pleasure. Each child is free to develop in the way and at the pace appropriate to his/her needs, abilities and interests. The school places special stress on individual discovery, on firsthand experience and on creative work.

At Kino Learning Center, adults and children mutually engaged in the learning process are continually in the process of changing and growing, for to learn is to change. And to experience joy in learning is to delight in life itself, for learning and life are one.

The curriculum at Kino Learning Center consists of teacher-made learning packets containing facts, processes and values related to topics of interest to the students. These learning packets have been expanded into workbooks for use by teachers and students throughout the United States and Europe. Over thirty books are presently in circulation. The profits from the sale of these books are used to enhance the learning environment at Kino Learning Center.

TABLE OF CONTENTS

	Page
INTRODUCTION	iv
PreTest	1
PART ONE: DECISIONS AFFECTING MY RELATIONSHIPS	2
Surveying My Values	2
Evaluating My Activities	5
Recognizing My Feelings	8
Working Through Problems	10
Determining Alternatives	13
Improving Quality of Life	14
Choosing Leisure	16
Choosing Success	19
Finding Balance	20
PART TWO: DECISIONS AFFECTING MY TIME	22
Charting My Day	22
Analyzing My Week	24
Organizing My Day	25
Setting and Accomplishing Goals	26
Knowing My Priorities	26
Stating My Goals	27
Creating a Plan of Action	28
Measuring My Success	30
Meeting with Success or Failure	31
PART THREE: DECISIONS AFFECTING MY HEALTH	32
Choosing My Foods	33
Eating Healthier	36
Using Drugs	38
Exercising	41
Relaxing My Body	43
Stimulating My Mind	44
Planning for Long Term Health	45
PART FOUR: DECISIONS AFFECTING MY FUTURE	47
Planning Ahead	47
Finding a Job	48
Creating Significant Change	50
Feeling Empowered	51
Looking Ahead	52
POSTTEST	58
STUDENT RESOURCES	59

INTRODUCTION
A MESSAGE TO STUDENTS

The road to adulthood is not without obstacles. You will take risks that will strengthen and shake your self-confidence. You will make decisions that will demonstrate both good and poor judgment. You will invest in relationships that will be both short-lived and long lasting. Some people will expect you to act older than you feel. Others will treat you like a child when you feel quite mature. All this can be quite confusing.

My Choices and Decisions is a workbook intended to assist you in your transition from adolescence to adulthood. The activities are designed to help you identify your thoughts and feelings, organize your life today and make optimistic plans for tomorrow.

This book is intended to help you view your road to adulthood as one that is paved with opportunities rather than obstacles. Your pace and direction is a personal choice. May your journey result in much happiness today and all the days ahead.

A MESSAGE TO TEACHERS

As adults, we most likely remember our adolescent years as a very stressful and threatening time in our lives. Adolescence is distressing because young people do not fully understand the many changes taking place in their lives. Many fears and anxieties could be reduced or eliminated by equipping young people with the skills to make responsible decisions. The activities in this book are designed to assist students to become more responsible decision makers and to demonstrate an increased awareness of the choices they make.

My Choices and Decisions allows students the opportunity to experience the art of choosing. Students will set daily goals and evaluate them. They will evaluate choices they are currently making and determine the reasons behind their choices. Students will problem solve by stating the problem, listing and evaluating alternatives, and determining consequences. Finally, students will consider choices that effect not only themselves but others around them today and in the years ahead.

As the activities in this book are completed, students will have repeated opportunities to affirm each other's uniqueness, capability and cooperation. This need for a positive self-image, a clearly defined values code, and consistent cooperative beliefs and behaviors is vital for today's youth as they begin to hold a more constructive and positive view of themselves and their world. Herein lies the challenge of the present moment and the hope for all that is worthwhile for generations to come.

• PRETEST

Before you begin *My Choices and Decisions*, complete the following statements by putting a check (✓) in the appropriate box.

		USUALLY	OFTEN	SOMETIMES	SELDOM	NEVER
RELATIONS	1. I am able to arrive at solutions to conflicts.					
	2. I consider the opinions of others when making decisions.					
	3. I give equal emphasis to self, others and work.					
TIME	4. I make responsible decisions regarding my time.					
	5. I set daily goals and try to accomplish them.					
	6. I identify problems and work toward solutions.					
HEALTH	7. I eat healthy food on a regular basis.					
	8. I vigorously exercise several times a week.					
	9. I make time for physical and mental relaxation.					
FUTURE	10. I believe I have the power to create my future.					
	11. I am developing the skills that are needed for my future employment.					
	12. I am hopeful about my future.					

Use the information stated above to make conclusions about your choices and decisions.

_____

_____

PART ONE: DECISIONS AFFECTING MY RELATIONSHIPS

PURPOSE

The decisions you make have a profound influence on the quality of your relationships. Part One is intended to help you determine the degree to which your values, attitudes and feelings affect your decision-making skills.

SURVEYING MY VALUES

Your values are those people and things that are important to you. Your values can best be determined by analyzing your feelings and actions.

Put a check (✓) in the box that best indicates your values.

		VERY TRUE	SOMEWHAT TRUE	SOMEWHAT FALSE	VERY FALSE
FAMILY	1. I enjoy doing things with my family.				
FAMILY	2. I enjoy spending an evening at home with my family.				
FAMILY	3. I am able to discuss my problems with my family.				
FRIENDS	4. I like to go places with my friends.				
FRIENDS	5. I share activities with friends.				
FRIENDS	6. I like being with people.				
MONEY	7. I think about owning an expensive car.				
MONEY	8. I would take a job I dislike for good pay.				
MONEY	9. I'd rather be rich than well liked.				

			VERY TRUE	SOMEWHAT TRUE	SOMEWHAT FALSE	VERY FALSE
RISK TAKING	10.	I would like to travel in outer space.				
	11.	I like to try things I've never done before.				
	12.	I like to take chances.				
BEAUTY	13.	I like beautiful scenery.				
	14.	I would like to own beautiful works of art.				
	15.	I enjoy music and art.				
CONTROL	16.	I would be President of the United States if I could.				
	17.	I like to take charge of a group.				
	18.	I like people to ask me for my opinion.				
KNOWLEDGE	19.	I know a lot about history.				
	20.	I like to learn new things.				
	21.	I like to attend interesting lectures.				
FREEDOM	22.	I would rather not answer to a boss.				
	23.	I like working by myself.				
	24.	I like to decide what to do and when to do it.				
COMMUNITY	25.	I like to help people.				
	26.	I think people should donate money to the poor.				
	27.	I would like a job that helps people.				
FAME	28.	I would like to be famous.				
	29.	I would like people to know that I've done something well.				
	30.	I would like to be on TV if I had the talent.				

Study the results of your survey. List those categories that were very true for you. These are the things you value the most.

_____

_____

_____

List those categories that were very false for you. These are the things you value the least.

_____

_____

_____

Discuss the results of your values survey with your teacher and classmates. Draw conclusions from the results of your survey.

_____

_____

_____

_____

_____

_____

_____

_____

_____

_____

_____

_____

_____

_____

_____

• EVALUATING MY ACTIVITIES

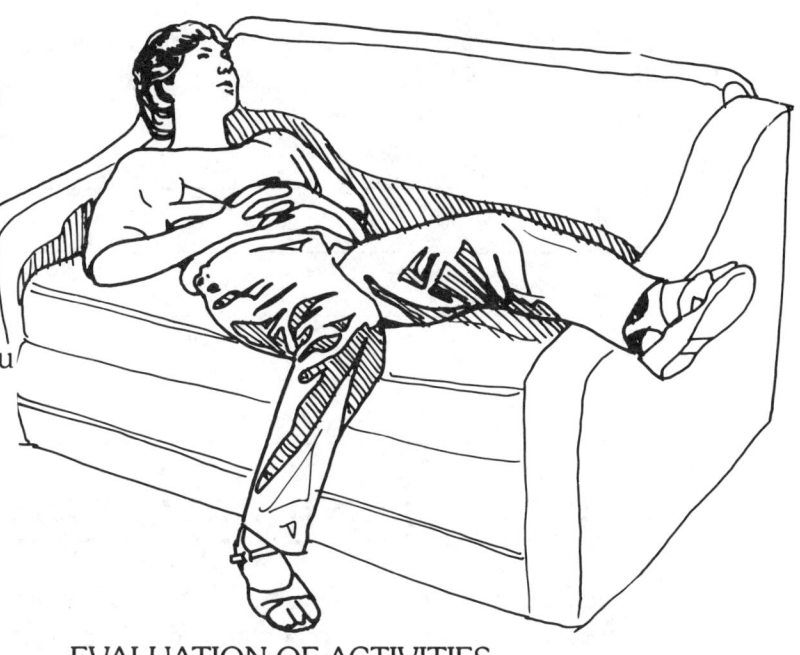

Your values affect your decisions. By identifying *what* you like to do and *why* you like to do it, you will be able to identify the values that determine your actions.

List ten things you like to do, such as play tennis, go to parties, etc., in the column below.

ACTIVITY

1. _____
2. _____
3. _____
4. _____
5. _____
6. _____
7. _____
8. _____
9. _____
10. _____

EVALUATION OF ACTIVITIES

W	WO	OS	IS	O	S	R	A	P	1	2	3

Use the following code to evaluate each activity. Record the proper code in the boxes after each activity.

W = activity done *with* people
WO = activity done *without* people

OS = activity done *outside*
IS = activity done *inside*

O = activity done *often*
S = activity done *sometimes*
R = activity done *rarely*

A = activity is *active*
P = activity is *passive*

1 = activity is *very important*
2 = activity is *somewhat important*
3 = activity is *not very important*

Study your evaluation results. Look for patterns regarding *what* you like to do and *why* you like to do it. Discuss your conclusions with your teacher and classmates. Record your conclusions below.

_____
_____
_____
_____
_____

• DETERMINING VALUES

Values are the people, things and activities that are important to you. A clear sense of what is important is needed to make informed decisions about your life.

Review your responses to Surveying My Values on pages 2-4 and Evaluating My Activities on page 5.

Name two *people* you value. Tell why you respect these people.

1. _____
   _____

2. _____
   _____

Name two *things* you value. Tell why these things are important to you.

1. _____
   _____

2. _____
   _____

Name two *activities* you value. Tell why you enjoy these activities.

1. _____
   _____

2. _____
   _____

MAKING DAILY DECISIONS

There are many important decisions that must be made in your lifetime. It is important to have the necessary values, attitudes and skills to make these decisions effectively.

Make a list of the ten most important decisions you make in a typical day.

_____ 1. _____
_____ 2. _____
_____ 3. _____
_____ 4. _____
_____ 5. _____
_____ 6. _____
_____ 7. _____
_____ 8. _____
_____ 9. _____
_____ 10. _____

Put a star (*) in front of your three most important decisions.

How many important decisions do you make in one day? _____

In one week? _____   In one month? _____   In one year? _____

Describe the attitudes, values and skills that qualify you to make important decisions in your life.

_____
_____
_____
_____
_____

• RECOGNIZING MY FEELINGS

Today's teenagers have more freedom and choices than ever before. Sometimes this may be confusing. It is important to know how you feel about various issues, since your feelings will dictate your actions regarding these issues.

Put a check (✓) in the column that best describes how you feel about the following statements.

	STRONGLY AGREE	AGREE	UNDECIDED	DISAGREE	STRONGLY DISAGREE
1. Boys need more education than girls.					
2. Men should not cry in public.					
3. Women are more sensitive than men.					
4. Occasional use of drugs will not cause a person harm.					
5. People who are alone are lonely people.					
6. Women with preschool children should not work outside the home.					
7. Men make better lawyers and doctors than women.					
8. Men should make more money than women holding the same job.					
9. Boys are smarter than girls.					
10. People on unemployment are lazy.					

Discuss your responses to these statements with a teacher whom you respect and admire.

Describe your responses below.

_____
_____
_____
_____
_____

• IMPROVING SITUATIONS

It is a great satisfaction to be able to identify a problem, determine a possible solution and implement this solution in a successful manner. Improving life's situations is a satisfying experience.

Describe a PERSONAL PROBLEM. Tell what you could do to improve this situation. Implement your plan for improvement.

_____
_____
_____
_____
_____
_____

Describe a LOCAL PROBLEM. Tell what you could do to improve this situation. Implement your plan for improvement.

_____
_____
_____
_____
_____
_____

Describe a NATIONAL or GLOBAL PROBLEM. Tell what you could do to improve this situation. Implement your plan for improvement.

_____
_____
_____
_____
_____
_____

• WORKING THROUGH PROBLEMS

You are aware of the frustration that results from being in conflict with family and friends. Being able to identify both sides of an issue is the first step to arriving at an equitable solution.

Read the situations below. Identify the conflicts and suggest equitable solutions.

Scenario #1	Going out at night with your friends is an important value. Your parents insist that you be home by 9:30 p.m. However, you want to stay out until 11:00 p.m.
My Goal:	_____
My Parents' Goal	_____
Our Solution to the Problem:	_____ _____ _____

Scenario #2	Many of your friends smoke. You have never tried it. Your friends joke about your being a goodie-goodie and offer you cigarettes.
My Goal:	_____
My Friend's Goal:	_____
Our Solution to the Problem:	_____ _____ _____

Scenario #3   Your physical education class changes in a large locker room. You are uncomfortable with this situation but want to resolve the conflict before the teacher or students notice your shyness.

My Goal: _____

My School's Goal: _____

Our Solution to the Problem: _____
_____
_____
_____

Scenario #4   A new student joins your class. You like him/her but your best friend does not want you to give this new person your time and attention.

My Goal: _____

My Friend's Goal: _____

Our Solution to the Problem: _____
_____
_____
_____

• SOLVING MY PROBLEMS

You can take greater charge of your life by setting goals, identifying obstacles to reaching these goals and determining solutions to these obstacles.

Describe situations in your life that need improvement.

My goal: _____
_____
_____

My problem: _____
_____
_____

My solution: _____
_____
_____

My goal: _____
_____
_____

My problem: _____
_____
_____

My solution: _____
_____
_____

Ask your teacher and classmates to help you further clarify your goal-setting and problem-solving techniques.

• DETERMINING ALTERNATIVES

Positive decision making involves looking at alternatives and assessing the advantages and disadvantages of each.

List two ways to accomplish the goals stated below. Indicate advantages and disadvantages for each suggestion.

Goal #1: To acquire new clothes

SUGGESTION FOR ACCOMPLISHING GOAL	ADVANTAGE OF SUGGESTION	DISADVANTAGE OF SUGGESTION

Goal #2: To enjoy the weekend

SUGGESTION FOR ACCOMPLISHING GOAL	ADVANTAGE OF SUGGESTION	DISADVANTAGE OF SUGGESTION

• IMPROVING QUALITY OF LIFE

Listed below are conveniences of modern living. Rank each invention as to its usefulness in improving the quality of your life and the lives of others.

1 = very useful
2 = somewhat useful
3 = not very useful
4 = not at all useful

_____ microwave oven
_____ communication satellite
_____ artificial heart
_____ electric toothbrush
_____ video telephone
_____ home security system
_____ personal computer
_____ solar water heater
_____ _____
_____ _____

Give reasons why you ranked these inventions as you did.

_____
_____
_____

Describe an invention you would develop to improve the quality of life for yourself and others.

_____
_____
_____
_____

• PAYING MY WAY

Being aware of your personal expenses is an important part of self-management. Becoming financially responsible is one aspect of growing to adulthood.

Estimate how much money you spend on clothing in a period of one year. Then determine the average amount you spend in one month. Record your figures below.

Type of Clothing	Number of Purchases	X	Average Cost per Item	=	TOTAL COST PER ITEM
		X	$	=	$
		X	$	=	$
		X	$	=	$
		X	$	=	$
		X	$	=	$
		X	$	=	$
		X	$	=	$
		X	$	=	$
		X	$	=	$

TOTAL COST PER YEAR $ _____

Determine your clothing cost per month by using the following formula:

TOTAL COST PER YEAR   ÷   12 MONTHS PER YEAR   =   AVERAGE COST PER MONTH

_____   ÷   _____   = $ _____

15

• CHOOSING LEISURE

The choices you make during your leisure time reflect your values.

Check (√) the word that best describes the statement.

I spend my leisure time

	USUALLY	OFTEN	SOMETIMES	SELDOM	NEVER
1. by myself.					
2. with my family.					
3. with friends.					
4. participating in sports.					
5. listening to music.					
6. watching television.					
7. reading books.					
8. doing nothing special.					
9.					
10.					

Based on your answers to these statements, draw conclusions regarding your values related to leisure time.

_____
_____
_____
_____
_____
_____

• PLANNING A GOOD TIME

You can take greater charge of your life by planning free time that is enjoyable, interesting and worthwhile.

Describe an exciting weekend in the space below.

Plan to make this dream weekend a reality in your life.

• AVOIDING PERSONAL GROWTH

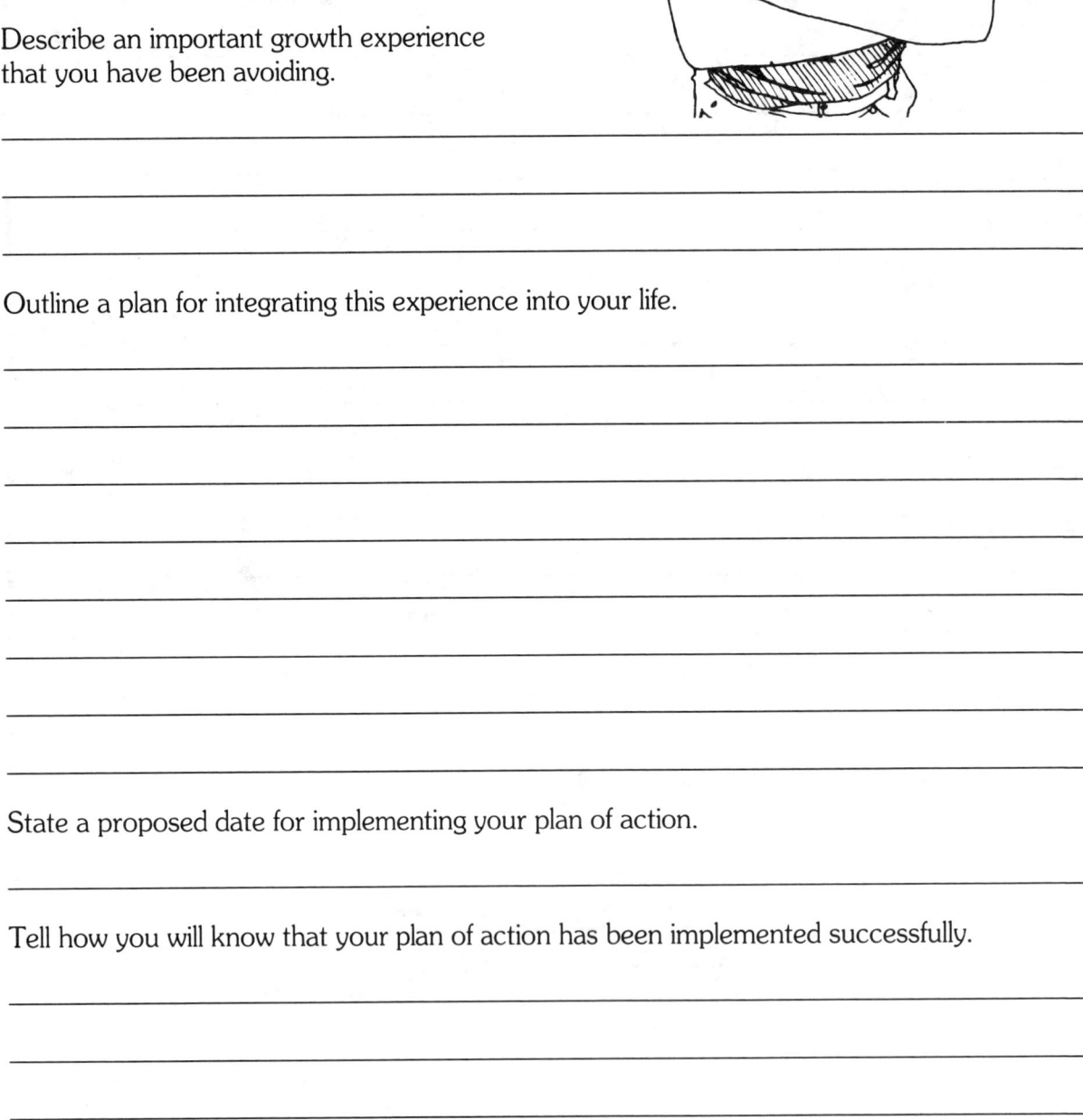

Not making a decision is a decision. It is common to have an area of growth that you tend to neglect. Avoiding personal growth results in an imbalance in your life.

Describe an important growth experience that you have been avoiding.

_____
_____
_____

Outline a plan for integrating this experience into your life.

_____
_____
_____
_____
_____
_____
_____

State a proposed date for implementing your plan of action.

_____

Tell how you will know that your plan of action has been implemented successfully.

_____
_____
_____

• CHOOSING SUCCESS

Tell about a decision you made that resulted in success.

_____
_____
_____
_____

Tell how you arrived at this decision.

_____
_____
_____

Describe the factors that contributed to your success.

_____
_____
_____
_____
_____
_____

Describe what you could have done to bring about a greater success related to this decision.

_____
_____
_____
_____
_____
_____

• FINDING BALANCE

A balanced person is one who gives equal emphasis to self, others and work. No one is in perfect balance all the time. It is important to realize, however, that balance is the key to happy, healthy living.

Read the descriptions and illustrate the degree of balance for each person.

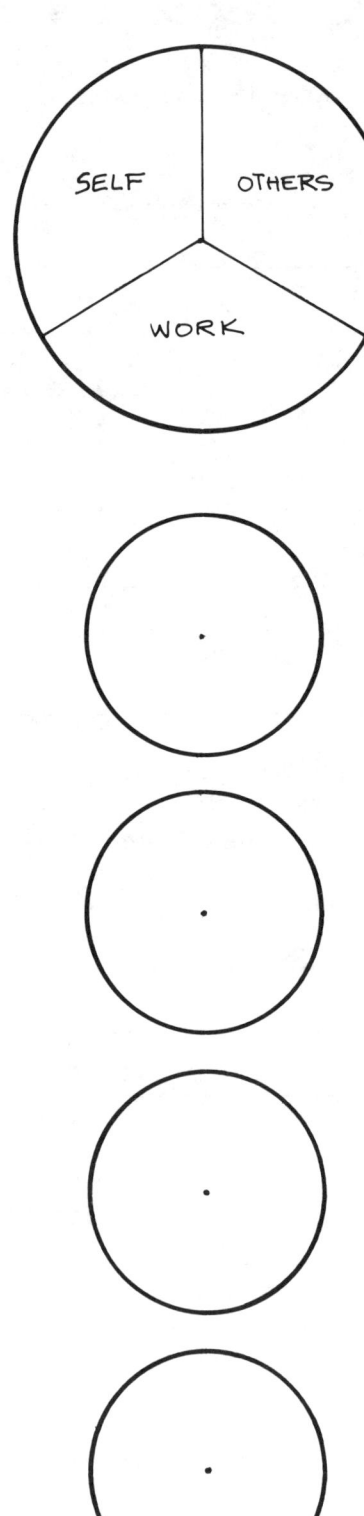

John never misses a day of school. He frequently exercises at the gym before going home to a supportive family.

Karen works very hard to keep good grades. In order to do so, she wears herself out and has little time to spend with her family or friends.

Barbara tries hard at school and volunteers for many service projects. Between classes and causes, she has little or no time for herself.

Bill is highly respected by everyone on the team. However, he sometimes skips school to develop his basketball skills and enjoy his friends.

Nancy often drinks in order to be popular with her friends. The "life of the party" frequently comes to school with a hangover.

Mike is very serious about his work and his hobbies, but he always finds time to enjoy his friends.

Jane has been very successful at her new job without neglecting her family or herself.

Describe yourself. Draw your balance profile.

_____
_____
_____
_____
_____
_____
_____

PART TWO: DECISIONS AFFECTING MY TIME

PURPOSE

The decisions you make affect the use of your time. Part Two is intended to help you evaluate your decisions in an effort to use your time efficiently and effectively.

• CHARTING MY DAY

Analyzing the time spent on daily activities will tell you a great deal about your values in life.

List your daily activities along the bottom of the graph. Fill in the graph to indicate the time spent on each activity. Repeat this procedure for a period of one week.

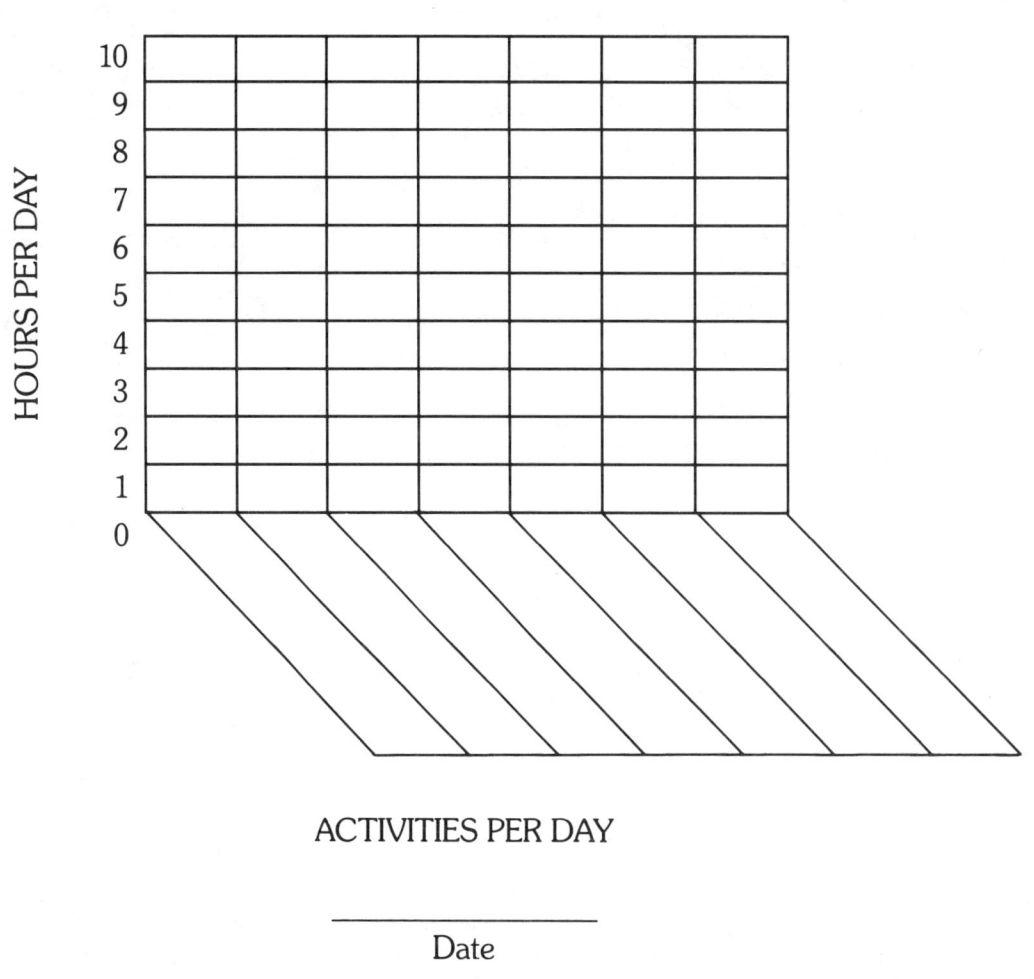

ACTIVITIES PER DAY

_____
Date

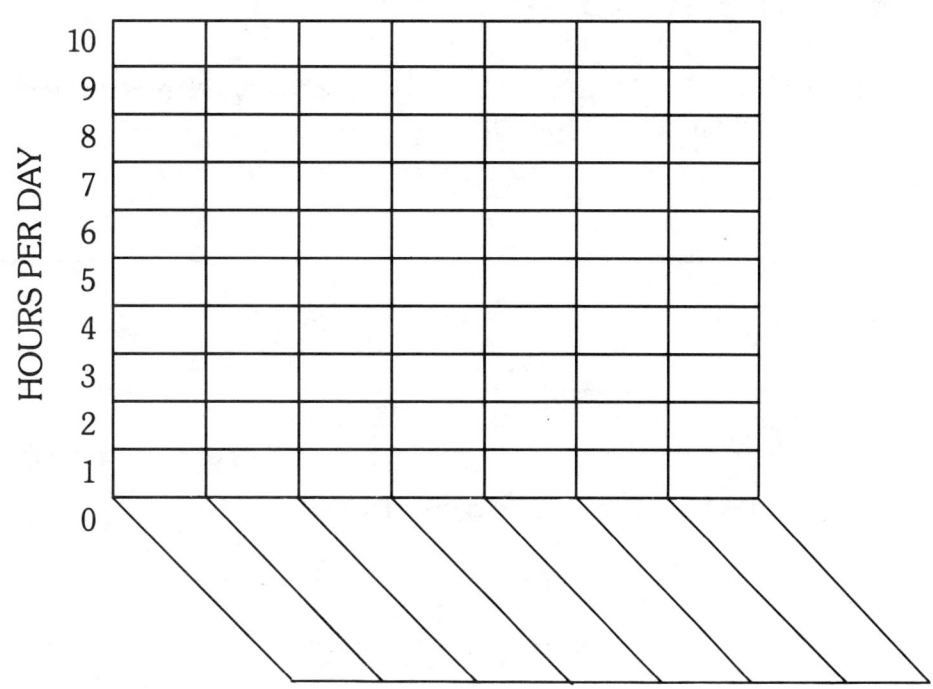

Date

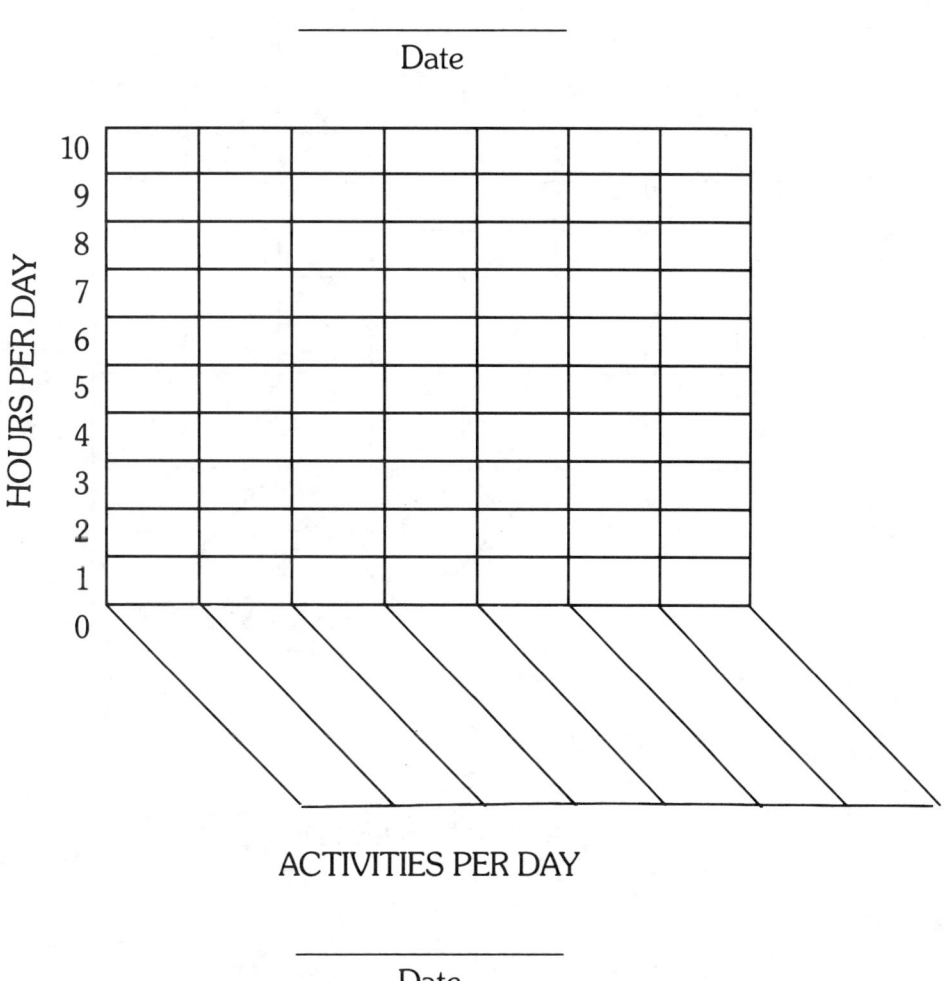

Date

• ANALYZING MY WEEK

Analyze the seven-bar graphs from the previous activity. Name those activities that consume the greatest amount of your time.

_____

_____

Name those activities that require the least amount of your time.

_____

_____

State what you could do to use your time more efficiently.

_____

_____

Chart the times and activities that would represent a balanced day. Discuss with your classmates why you believe the graph depicts a balanced day.

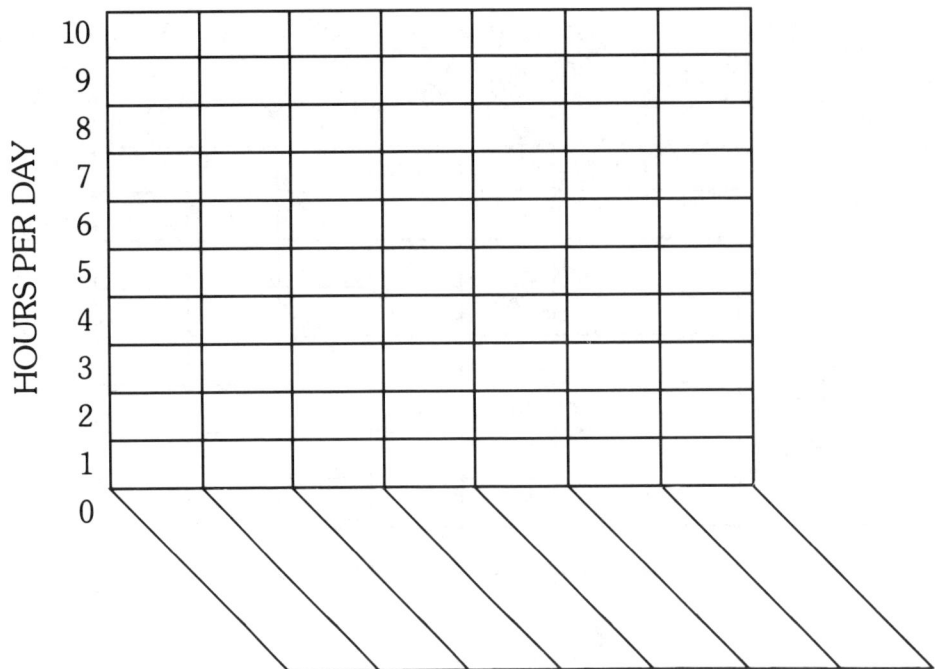

ACTIVITIES PER DAY

_____
Date

24

• ORGANIZING MY DAY

List the activities you intend to accomplish in a day. Number each activity from the most (1) to the least (10) important. Put a check (✓) in the box when your goal has been completed.

MY GOALS TODAY

Name _____ Date _____

Rank of Goal	Activity	Goal Completed
_____	_____	☐
_____	_____	☐
_____	_____	☐
_____	_____	☐
_____	_____	☐
_____	_____	☐
_____	_____	☐
_____	_____	☐
_____	_____	☐
_____	_____	☐

SETTING AND ACCOMPLISHING GOALS

Successfully setting and accomplishing your goals involves 1) knowing your priorities, 2) stating your goals, 3) creating a plan to complete these goals, and 4) evaluating the success of your plan.

Examine the four steps of goal setting described below.

Step 1: KNOWING MY PRIORITIES

Your priorities reflect your values. Your values are those people and things that are important to you. Your priorities can be determined by analyzing your feelings and behaviors.

Put a *1* next to those activities that are *very important* to you, a *2* next to those activities that are *somewhat important* and a *3* next to those activities that are *not very important*.

_____ spending time with my family.

_____ being free to make my own decisions.

_____ having friends.

_____ being alone.

_____ taking risks.

_____ spending money.

_____ traveling and seeing new places.

_____ helping other people.

_____ doing things outdoors.

_____ working with groups.

Review your responses. Draw conclusions regarding your priorities in life.

_____

_____

_____

Step 2: STATING MY GOALS

A goal is a statement of a desired achievement. Goals reflect values. Once a goal has been stated, plans can be made to achieve it.

1. **MY PERSONAL GOAL:**

    State a goal that would enhance your personal life.

    _____
    _____
    _____
    _____

2. **MY SOCIAL GOAL:**

    State a goal that would enhance your social life.

    _____
    _____
    _____
    _____

3. **MY ACADEMIC GOAL:**

    State a goal that would enhance your academic life.

    _____
    _____
    _____
    _____

4. **MY FUTURE GOAL:**

    State a goal that would enhance your future.

    _____
    _____
    _____
    _____

Step 3: CREATING A PLAN OF ACTION

A plan of action consists of *objectives*. An objective is a statement of a specific activity to be completed within a specific time period in order to accomplish the desired goal.

State a plan of action for accomplishing each goal in Step 2. (Note: Make sure that each objective states an action and a time frame in which to complete the action.)

PERSONAL PLAN OF ACTION

1. GOAL: _____

_____

Objectives to accomplish this goal:

1. _____
2. _____

SOCIAL PLAN OF ACTION

2. GOAL: _____

_____

Objectives to accomplish this goal:

1. _____
2. _____

ACADEMIC PLAN OF ACTION

3. GOAL: _____
_____

Objectives to accomplish this goal:

1. _____
2. _____

FUTURE PLAN OF ACTION

4. GOAL: _____
_____

Objectives to accomplish this goal:

1. _____
2. _____

Discuss with your teacher and classmates a plan of action for improving a situation in your classroom or school. State your plan for improvement below.

MY PLAN OF ACTION

GOAL: _____
_____

Objectives to accomplish this goal:

1. _____
_____
2. _____
_____

Step 4: MEASURING MY SUCCESS

Once sufficient effort has been made to achieve a goal, it is important to evaluate the degree of success of your efforts.

Restate one goal from Step 2:

Goal: _____

_____

Check (✓) the appropriate response regarding your degree of success in accomplishing this goal.

1. My degree of success in accomplishing this goal was:

    ____ very high.

    ____ rather high.

    ____ rather low.

    ____ very low.

2. The activities stated in the objectives were:

    ____ clearly stated and attainable.

    ____ clearly stated but unattainable.

    ____ unclear and unattainable.

3. My time line for accomplishing this goal was:

    ____ realistic.

    ____ too long.

    ____ too short.

4. One way to accomplish greater success might be:

_____

_____

_____

Note: Repeat this evaluation procedure for the remaining goals stated in Step 2.

• MEETING WITH SUCCESS OR FAILURE

Have you ever wondered what makes some people more successful than others? Talents and abilities are important, but equally important is knowing what you want and consciously choosing actions that will lead toward your goal.

State a goal that you have failed to accomplish in your life.
_____
_____

State factors that led to the failure of this goal.
_____
_____
_____

State what might have been done to make this goal more successful.
_____
_____
_____

State a goal that you have successfully accomplished in your life.
_____
_____

State factors that contributed to the success of this goal.
_____
_____
_____

State what might have been done to make this goal more successful.
_____
_____
_____

PART THREE: DECISIONS AFFECTING MY HEALTH

PURPOSE

Good health consists of sound nutrition, physical fitness, quality relationships, intellectual stimulation and a clearly defined value system. Part Three is intended to help you make sound decisions regarding your physical health and general well-being.

• ASSESSING MY HEALTH

Your physical health and well-being are affected by your daily decisions. You are in control of your eating, exercising and relaxing.

Check (√) the word that best fits the statement.

I make decisions

	USUALLY	OFTEN	SOMETIMES	SELDOM	NEVER
1. to eat nutritional foods on a regular basis.					
2. to exercise vigorously and regularly.					
3. to care for my long term health.					
4. to avoid drugs that may affect my well-being.					
5. to get enough sleep.					
6. to relax my mind and body.					
7. to care for my personal hygiene.					

• CHOOSING MY FOODS

The types of foods you choose influence the way you feel. A balanced diet is necessary for the development of a healthy body.

Listed below are the four food groups: meat, milk, grains, fruits and vegetables. Record the foods that you eat throughout the day in the proper food group category.

	MEAL	FOOD GROUPS			
		MEAT	MILK	GRAINS	FRUIT & VEG.
DAY 1	Breakfast				
	Lunch				
	Dinner				
	Snacks				
DAY 2	Breakfast				
	Lunch				
	Dinner				
	Snacks				
DAY 3	Breakfast				
	Lunch				
	Dinner				
	Snacks				
DAY 4	Breakfast				
	Lunch				
	Dinner				
	Snacks				

| | MEAL | FOOD GROUPS ||||
		MEAT	MILK	GRAINS	FRUIT & VEG.
DAY 5	Breakfast				
	Lunch				
	Dinner				
	Snacks				
DAY 6	Breakfast				
	Lunch				
	Dinner				
	Snacks				
DAY 7	Breakfast				
	Lunch				
	Dinner				
	Snacks				

Review the information that you recorded about your diet. Determine ways to improve your diet. State these goals in the space below.

_____
_____
_____
_____
_____
_____
_____
_____
_____

OBSERVING MY EATING HABITS

How you eat is as important as *what* you eat. Your eating habits and patterns contribute to or detract from your health and well-being.

Put an *X* on the continuum that best describes your general eating habits.

I eat when I am hungry. •——•——•——•——• I eat when I am bored.

I eat in a calm, relaxed environment. •——•——•——•——• I eat in a hectic environment with many distractions.

I eat sitting down. •——•——•——•——• I eat on the run.

I eat slowly and deliberately. •——•——•——•——• I eat quickly and without concentrating.

I stop eating when I am full. •——•——•——•——• I eat far after I am full.

I eat balanced, nutritious meals. •——•——•——•——• I pay no attention to what I eat.

• EATING HEALTHIER

Eating well involves choosing the right food and developing good eating habits.

The information you gathered in the two previous activities gives you an overview of your eating choices.

Think of ways to improve your eating patterns. Write these suggestions below.

NEEDED CHANGES IN MY DIET	ACTIONS I WILL TAKE TO BRING ABOUT CHANGE
example: to eat more grain	I will eat bran cereal three times a week for breakfast.

• MEASURING MY ENERGY LEVEL

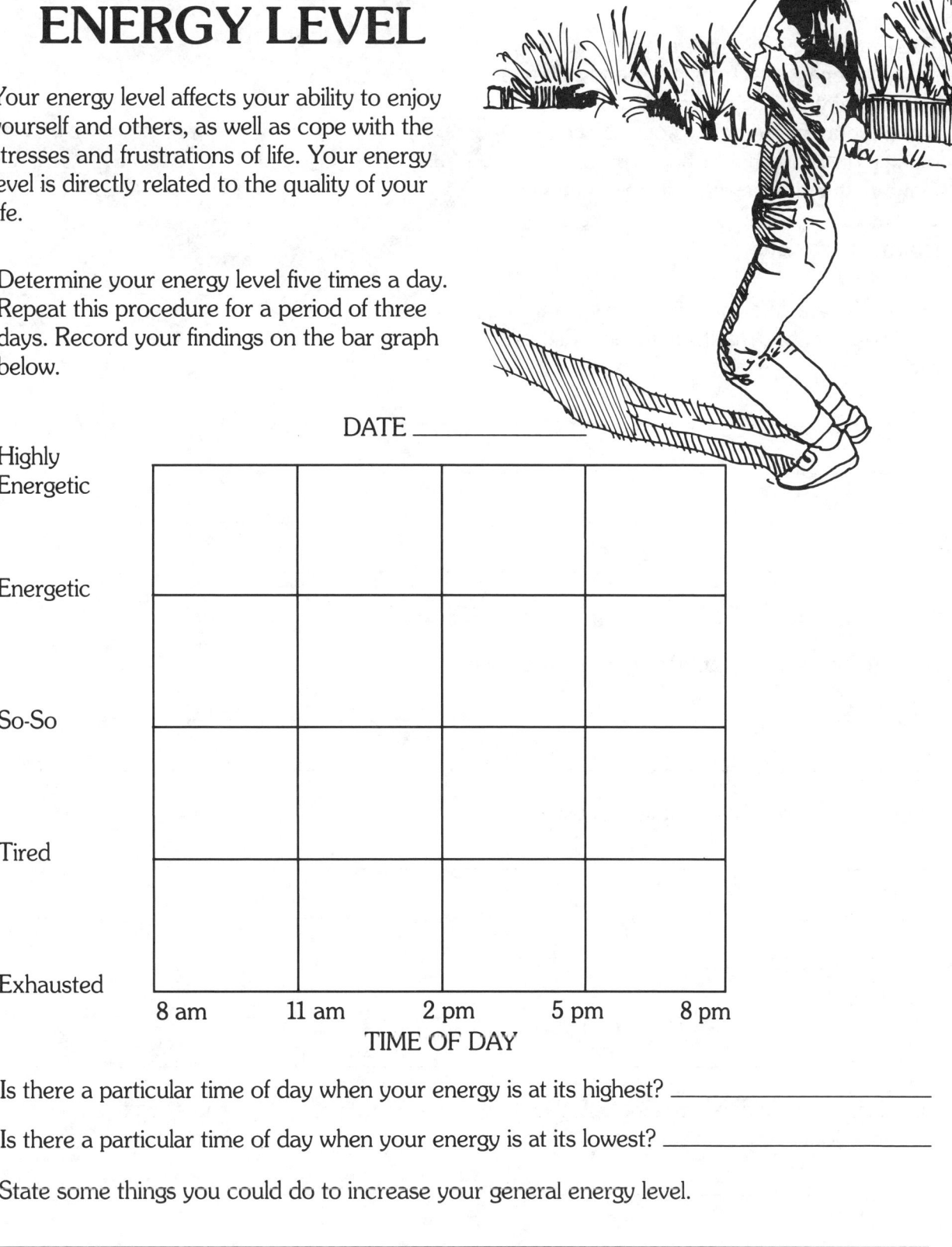

Your energy level affects your ability to enjoy yourself and others, as well as cope with the stresses and frustrations of life. Your energy level is directly related to the quality of your life.

Determine your energy level five times a day. Repeat this procedure for a period of three days. Record your findings on the bar graph below.

DATE _____

Highly Energetic

Energetic

So-So

Tired

Exhausted

| 8 am | 11 am | 2 pm | 5 pm | 8 pm |

TIME OF DAY

Is there a particular time of day when your energy is at its highest? _____

Is there a particular time of day when your energy is at its lowest? _____

State some things you could do to increase your general energy level.

_____
_____

• USING DRUGS

The availability of drugs is a fact of life for today's teenagers. The choices and decisions you make regarding drugs may affect the rest of your life. Someday you will need to make a decision about using drugs. Gathering and reviewing information about various drugs will allow you to make an informed decision.

Obtain general information about a common drug (i.e., alcohol, marijuana, crack, diet pills, etc.).

_____
_____
_____
_____
_____

State the possible advantages of using this drug.

_____
_____

State the possible disadvantages of using this drug.

_____
_____

State possible consequences of using this drug.

_____
_____

Decide if you would experiment with this drug, use this drug regularly or not use this drug at all. State your decision below.

_____
_____

• CARING FOR MY BODY

Your body requires proper care and attention. As a teenager, you may notice that your skin is oily. You or your friends may begin to get acne. Your body odor may begin to change. All of these changes are natural functions of growing older. Establishing a program for personal hygiene is important in caring for your body and in helping you feel good about yourself.

Listed below are several methods of personal hygiene. Fill in the chart with the appropriate information.

METHOD OF HYGIENE	WHAT I AM DOING	WHAT MORE I COULD DO
1. washing my face		
2. taking a shower/bath		
3. brushing my teeth		
4. flossing my teeth		
5. washing my hair		
6. using deodorant		

• PROMOTING PRODUCTS

The media promotes many items for personal hygiene. Some of these items may be useful to you. Many of these items will be of no value to you.

Create a collage of magazine advertisements that promote useful items for personal hygiene.

• EXERCISING

Good physical condition is achieved and maintained through a regular exercise program. A worthwhile physical fitness program consists of strength, endurance and flexibility.

Record the type of exercise and the number of minutes you do each exercise in a day. Keep this record for a period of one week.

DAY	S-E-F	TYPE OF EXERCISE	Number of minutes
1			
2			
3			
4			
5			
6			
7			

TOTAL MINUTES _____

Put an *S* before each activity that promotes *strength,* an *E* before each that promotes *endurance* and an *F* before each that promotes *flexibility.*

How many hours per day do you exercise? _____

How many hours per week? _____

Check one.

The amount of time I exercise is:

☐ very adequate.

☐ somewhat adequate.

☐ inadequate.

Discuss the strengths of your exercise program.

_____
_____
_____
_____

Discuss the weaknesses of your exercise program.

_____
_____
_____
_____

Revise and strengthen your current exercise program. Include exercises that develop strength, flexibility and endurance. Tell about your revised program in the space below.

_____
_____
_____
_____
_____
_____

• RELAXING MY BODY

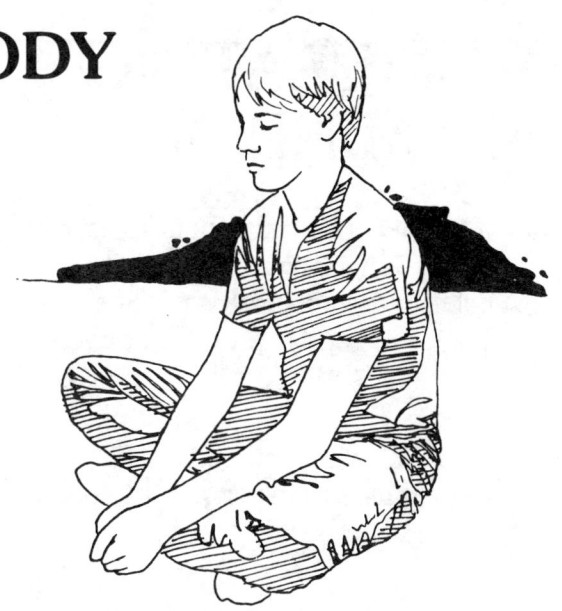

Relaxation of the body is important to maintaining wellness. When your body is tense or tired, problems appear to be magnified and decisions can be made without proper thought. Relaxation enhances clear thinking.

Tape-record the following relaxation exercise. Play it every day for a period of one week.

Sit back and make yourself comfortable. Allow your eyelids to close. Become conscious of your body's growing relaxation. Imagine yourself as a leaf floating peacefully to Earth. Feel the muscles relaxing in your scalp . . . your face . . . your neck . . . shoulders . . . arms . . . and hands. Continue floating to Earth. Breathe easily, with each breath becoming relaxed and free of tension. Relax your chest . . . stomach . . . abdomen. Be calm and comfortable. Let go of all your problems. Continue floating to the ground. Relax your legs and feet. Drift comfortably . . . deeper . . . deeper . . . until you rest gently on the ground. Enjoy the calmness . . . enjoy the quiet . . . enjoy the peace.

When you are ready, rise up.

Carry your feelings with you as you continue your day.

Describe other methods you use to relax your body. Tell how frequently you use these methods.

_____
_____
_____
_____
_____
_____
_____
_____

• STIMULATING MY MIND

Development of your mind results in clear, quick thinking. Choosing activities that purposefully sharpen your senses helps you develop your mind and improve your overall quality of life.

The activities below are intended to help you develop your senses of hearing, sight, touch, taste and smell.

HEARING	Listen to a sporting event on the radio. Imagine you are at the event.
SEEING	Watch your favorite television show with the sound off. Try to "hear" with your eyes.
TOUCHING	Touch your way through a normal day. Wear a blindfold while completing your daily activities.
TASTING	With your eyes blindfolded, taste several different types of food. Try to identify them.
SMELLING	With your eyes blindfolded, smell pleasant odors. Try to identify these smells.

Describe the usefulness of the activities stated above.

_____
_____
_____
_____

Design your own activity that will sharpen your senses and your mind.

_____
_____
_____
_____

• PLANNING FOR LONG TERM HEALTH

The choices you make today affect your degree of happiness and success in the future. Choosing balance and working toward excellence are important to your long term growth and development.

Listed below are the four areas related to successful living: personal success, financial success, good health and educational success. Rank yourself in these areas using the scale below:

1 = highly successful

2 = somewhat successful

3 = not successful

AREAS FOR SUCCESSFUL LIVING	RANK
FINANCES Financial success involves the development of useful skills for employment and proper management of personal money.	
HEALTH Wellness involves being in good physical and mental health, as well as developing the skills to make choices that promote happiness.	
PERSONAL DEVELOPMENT Personal Development involves the formation of long lasting relationships, as well as a good self-concept.	
EDUCATIONAL/PROFESSIONAL DEVELOPMENT Educational/Professional Development involves working to the best of one's ability, as well as being respected by others and contributing to society.	

• AREAS FOR SUCCESSFUL LIVING

Rank your four areas of successful living stated on page 45. Shade the center area for a rank of 1. Shade the center and middle areas for a rank of 2. Shade the center, middle and outer areas for a rank of 3.

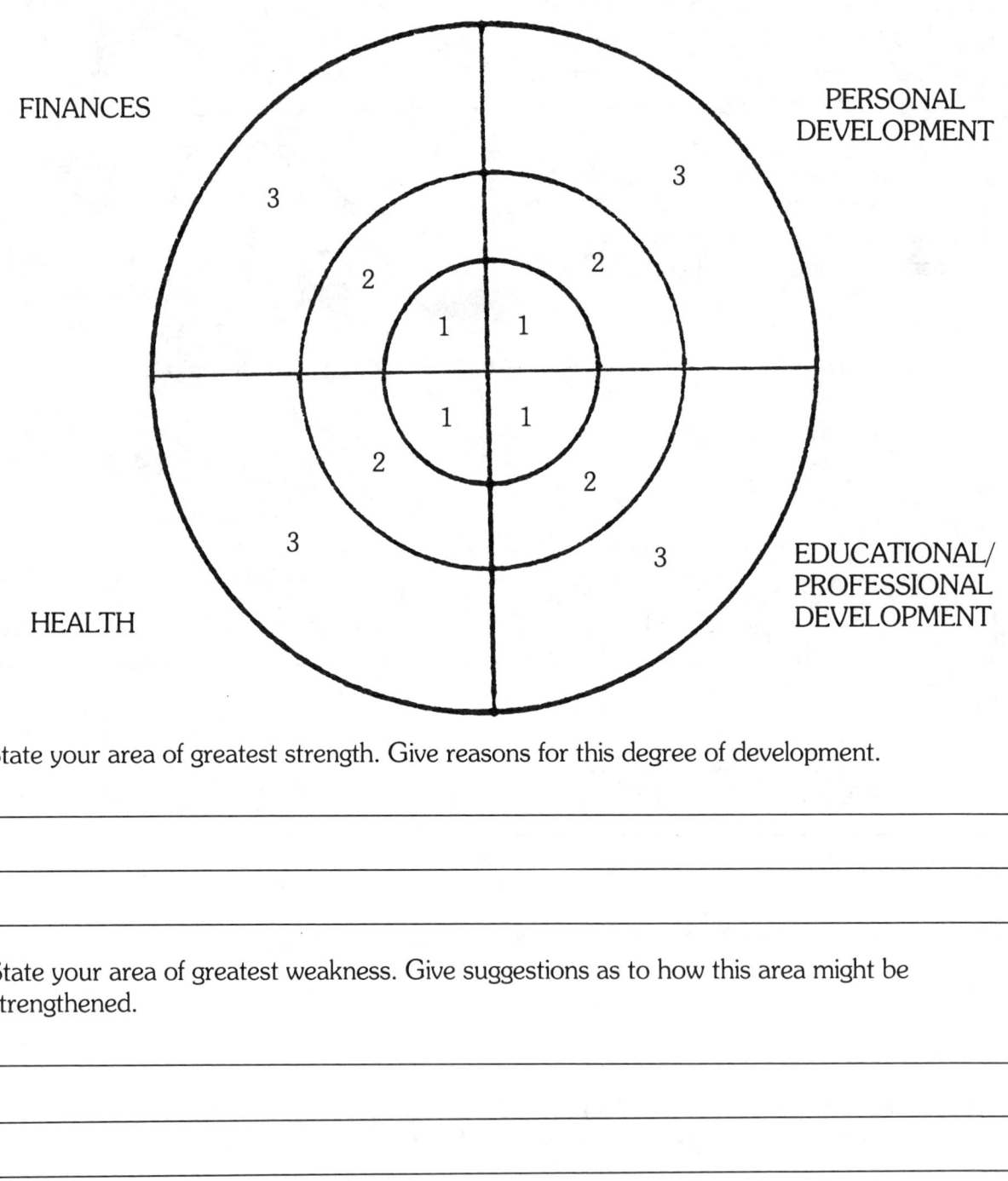

State your area of greatest strength. Give reasons for this degree of development.

_____
_____
_____

State your area of greatest weakness. Give suggestions as to how this area might be strengthened.

_____
_____
_____
_____

PART FOUR: DECISIONS AFFECTING MY FUTURE

PURPOSE

The decisions you make regarding your relationships, time and health have a profound effect upon the quality of your life. Part Four is intended to help you effectively apply your decision-making skills to your future.

• PLANNING AHEAD

Unfortunately, many teenagers do not have a clear picture of their immediate or distant future. It is important to look ahead, since planning is the first step to creating your future.

Interview a friend regarding his/her immediate and distant future. Record these responses below.

Name _____ Age _____ M or F

What are your plans after high school?

_____

_____

What do you think you will be doing at age 30?

_____

_____

What do you think you will be doing at age 50?

_____

_____

Discuss the above responses with your teacher and classmates. Is the interviewee making adequate, immediate plans? Is this person making adequate, distant plans?

● FINDING A JOB

There are various resources available to help you find a job. You could consult the *Occupational Outlook Handbook* from the U. S. Department of Labor. You could interview at a career center in your town. Or, you could consult the classified advertising section of newspapers in cities of interest to you.

Consult the classified section of your local newspaper. Cut out employment ads for jobs in which you are *interested* and *qualified*. Glue these ads in the space below.

Cut out employment ads for jobs in which you are *interested* but *not qualified*. Glue these ads in the space below.

```
┌─────────────────────────────────────────────────────┐
│                                                     │
│                                                     │
│                                                     │
│                                                     │
│                                                     │
│                                                     │
│                                                     │
│                                                     │
│                                                     │
│                                                     │
│                                                     │
└─────────────────────────────────────────────────────┘
```

Circle the job of greatest interest to you. Tell what you would have to do to qualify for this job.

_____

_____

_____

CREATING SIGNIFICANT CHANGE

In order to significantly influence the future, you must understand the present. You must know what you want to retain and what you want to change about the present. Clearly understanding the problems of today is the first step to creating a better tomorrow.

Research a major contemporary problem. State possible ways to reduce or eliminate this problem in the future. (Note: Some modern day problems are acid rain, air or water pollution, endangered animals, toxic waste disposal, overpopulation, unemployment, homeless people, etc.)

Contemporary problem:
_____
_____

Information related to problem:
_____
_____
_____
_____
_____
_____
_____
_____

Ways to reduce or eliminate problem:
_____
_____
_____
_____

• FEELING EMPOWERED

When you feel empowered, you believe you have the ability to create an optimistic future. Powerlessness, real or imagined, adds to your inability to create an optimistic future.

Survey twelve people. Ask each person if he/she has TOTAL POWER, SOME POWER, LITTLE POWER or NO POWER to create his/her future. Check (✓) each response in the space below.

PERSON	HAS TOTAL POWER	HAS SOME POWER	HAS LITTLE POWER	HAS NO POWER
1				
2				
3				
4				
5				
6				
7				
8				
9				
10				
11				
12				

What conclusions can you draw from your survey?

_____

_____

_____

_____

• LOOKING AHEAD

Pages 52 through 56 indicate a 100-year time line marked at 10-year intervals. Provide the information indicated. Hang your time line in a place of importance.

Paste your baby picture here.	Paste a recent photograph here.

Age _____   Age _____

Date of Birth   10 years

_____

Tell about the earliest thing you remember.	Tell what you like the most about your present school days.

Glue the left side of page 53 along this dotted line.

52

Draw the house where you someday plan to live.

Give the following information regarding your future place of residence.

_____
Street

_____
City

_____
State

_____
Country

20 years   30 years

Describe the type of further education you plan to receive.

Describe the jobs you will have as an adult.

Glue the left side of page 54 along this dotted line.

53

Tell about your future family and friends.

_____
_____
_____
_____
_____
_____
_____
_____
_____

Paste a photo of a person whom you respect here.

I respect _____

because _____
_____
_____
_____

40 years   50 years   60 years

Put an O on the places you have visited.
Put an X on the places you plan to visit.

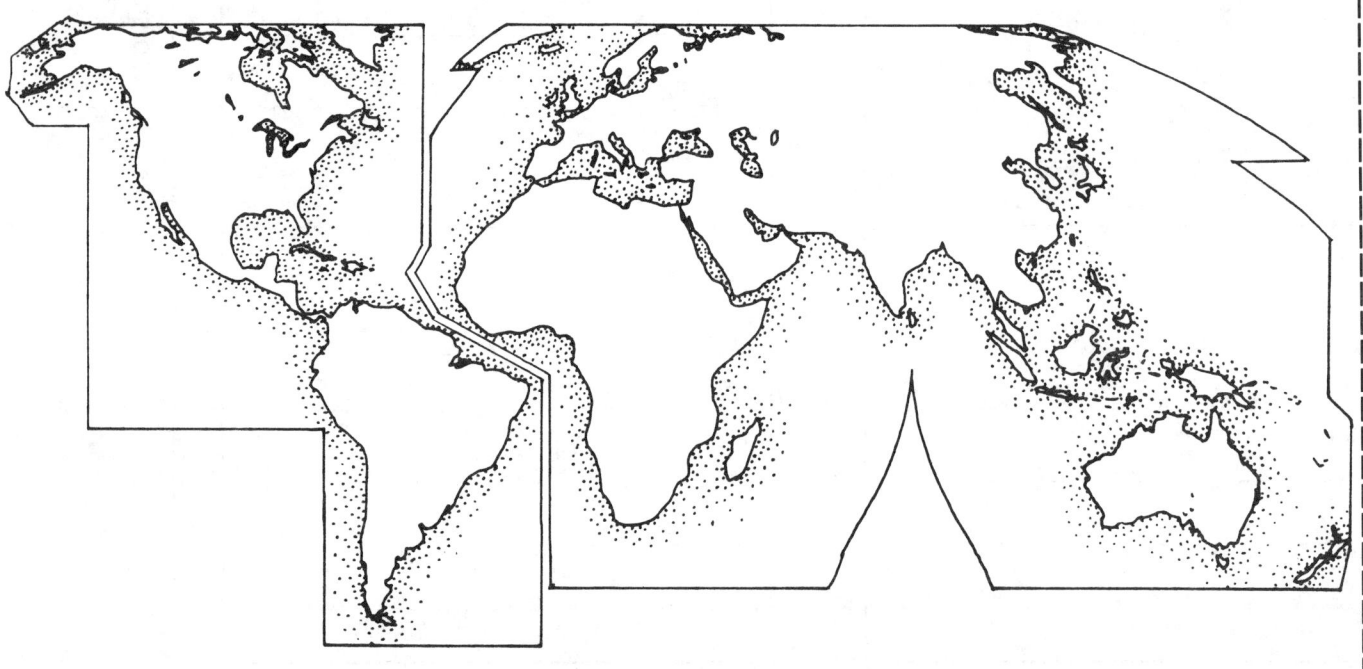

Glue the left side of page 55 along this dotted line.

Use magazine pictures to create a collage that represents you.

70 years   80 years

Describe a recurring fear or worry.

Describe what you plan to do for relaxation and enjoyment.

Glue the left side of page 56 along this dotted line.

| Tell what you value most in life. | Tell when and how you will die. |

90 years   100 years

| Tell what you plan to do to make the world a better place in which to live. | Tell what you hope will be said about you at your funeral. |

• IMAGINING THE FUTURE

Creating the future in your mind is the first step to making this dream a reality.

Tell about a yet unaccomplished dream.

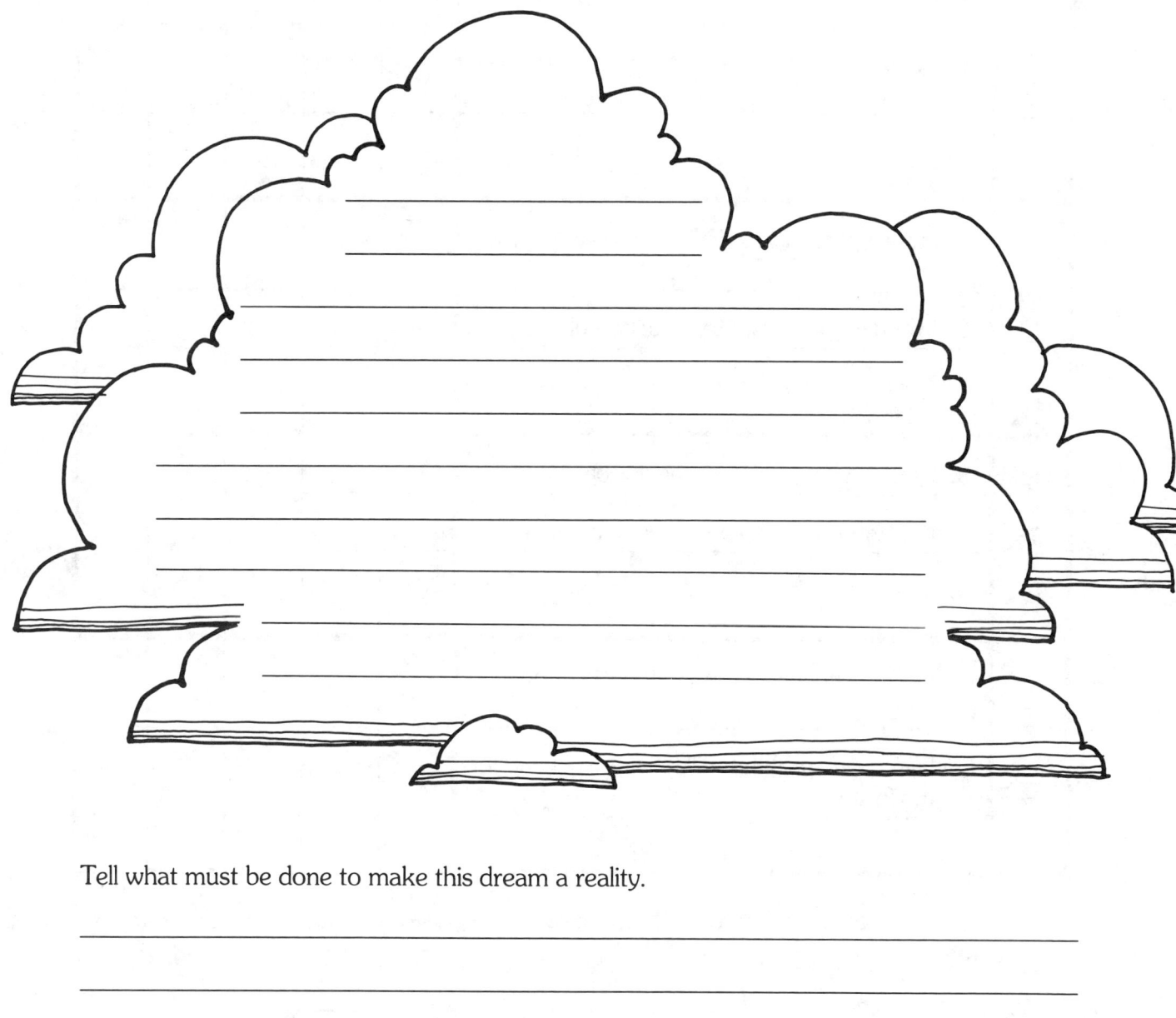

Tell what must be done to make this dream a reality.

_____
_____
_____
_____
_____

Put your dream plan into action.

• POSTTEST

Now that you have completed *My Choices and Decisions*, complete the following statements by putting a check (✓) in the appropriate box.

		USUALLY	OFTEN	SOMETIMES	SELDOM	NEVER
RELATIONSHIPS	1. I am able to arrive at solutions to conflicts.					
	2. I consider the opinions of others when making decisions.					
	3. I give equal emphasis to self, others and work.					
TIME	4. I make responsible decisions regarding my time.					
	5. I set daily goals and try to accomplish them.					
	6. I identify problems and work toward solutions.					
HEALTH	7. I eat healthy food on a regular basis.					
	8. I vigorously exercise several times a week.					
	9. I make time for physical and mental relaxation.					
FUTURE	10. I believe I have the power to create my future.					
	11. I am developing the skills that are needed for my future employment.					
	12. I am hopeful about my future.					

Compare your pretest and posttest responses. State possible reasons for any changes in your responses.

_____

_____

_____

_____

STUDENT RESOURCES

Bingham, Edmondson, Stryker. *Choices: A Teen Woman's Journal for Self-Awareness and Personal Planning.* Santa Barbara, California: Advocacy Press, 1983.

An activity book for young women containing exercises that help a person understand herself, her relationships, her interests and her future.

Bingham, Edmondson, Stryker. *Challenges: A Young Man's Journal for Self-Awareness and Personal Planning.* Santa Barbara, California: Advocacy Press, 1984.

An activity book for young men containing exercises that help a person understand himself, his relationships, his interests and his future.

Bisignano, Bisignano, Sanders. *Creating Your Future: Activities to Encourage Thinking Ahead.* Kansas City, Missouri: Sheed and Ward, 1982.

Designed to help students develop and improve their skills of choosing, relating, creating, valuing and learning how to learn. Focuses on changes that are and will occur in the student's relationships, lifestyle, political world, future, etc.

Sanders, Corinne. *Coping.* Carthage, Illinois: Good Apple, 1982.

Exercises that encourage analysis and evaluation of present methods of coping with stress. Guides exploration of alternative solutions to problems and examines indications of stress. Offers a means of managing stress through the development of a balanced lifestyle.

Sanders, Corinne. *Choosing.* Carthage, Illinois: Good Apple, 1985.

Exercises and experiences to help children make choices according to their internal values systems.